GUIDE TO
BRAZIL

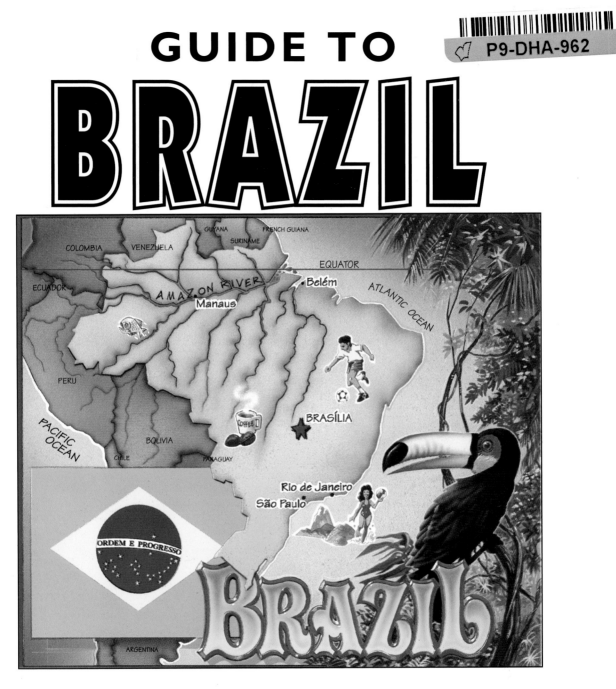

COLOMBIA
VENEZUELA
GUYANA
SURINAME
FRENCH GUIANA
EQUATOR
ECUADOR
AMAZON RIVER
Belém
ATLANTIC OCEAN
Manaus
PERU
PACIFIC OCEAN
COFFEE
BRASÍLIA
BOLIVIA
CHILE
PARAGUAY
Rio de Janeiro
São Paulo
ORDEM E PROGRESSO
ARGENTINA
BRAZIL

MARION MORRISON

Highlights for Children

CONTENTS

On the cover: Copacabana Beach with Sugarloaf Mountain in the background, two world-famous landmarks of the city of Rio de Janeiro

The publisher is grateful for the assistance of Benny Zadik in reviewing this book. Mr. Zadik is a graduate student in the Latin American Studies program at the University of California at Berkeley. Fluent in Portuguese, he is a writer and a translator based in San Francisco, California.

Published by Highlights for Children
© 1995 Highlights for Children, Inc.
P.O. Box 18201
Columbus, Ohio 43218-0201
For information on *Top Secret Adventures*, visit
www.tsadventures.com or call 1-800-962-3661.

14 13 12   HPS

ISBN 0-87534-917-X

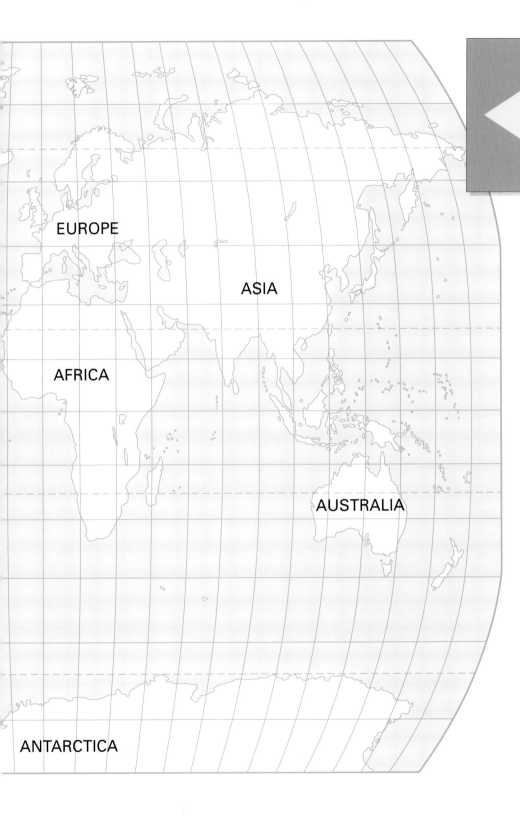

EUROPE

ASIA

AFRICA

AUSTRALIA

ANTARCTICA

△ **Brazilian Flag**
The stars on the globe represent the states and the original capital. The motto means "Order and Progress." The color green stands for Brazil's fields and forests, yellow for its gold, and blue for the sky.

BRAZIL AT A GLANCE

Area 3,285,630 square miles (8,511,996 square kilometers)

Population 198,739,269

Capital Brasília, population 2,455,903

Other big cities São Paulo (population 18,333,000), Rio de Janeiro (11,469,000), Salvador (2,590,400)

Highest mountain Pico da Neblina 9,889 feet (3,014 meters)

Longest river Amazon, 4,025 miles (6,690 kilometers); section crossing Brazil almost 1,800 miles (2,830 kilometers)

Largest lake Lagoa dos Patos 3,802 square miles (9,850 square kilometers)

Official language Portuguese

▽ **Brazilian stamps** Some feature children. Others show Brazilian wildlife and fish, coffee (Brazil's number-one crop), and the country's love of music and dancing.

▷ **Brazilian money** Brazil's currency is the Real, or R$. One Real=100 centavos.

VENEZUELA

GUYANA

SURINAME

FRENCH GUIANA

▲ Pico da Neblina

Negro

Amazon

Amazon

Madeira

Acre

Tapajós

Rondônia

Mato Grosso

Araguaia

Xingu

Serra dos Carajás

Ilha de Marajó

Belém

São Luis

ATLANTIC OCEAN

N
W E
S

Fortaleza

Tucuruí Dam

Juàzeiro do Norte

Goiana

Olinda

Recife

São Francisco

Penedo

Tocantins

Parnaíba

Ilha do Bananal

Manaus

Cuiabá

BOLIVIA

Corumbá

Campo Grande

Paraná

PARAGUAY

Itaipu Dam

Iguaçu Falls

Iguaçu

Paraná

CHILE

Brasília ★

Minas Gerais

Belo Horizonte

Rio de Janeiro

São Paulo

▲ Sugarloaf Mountain

Copacabana

Curitiba

Rio Negro

Santa Catarina

Bahia

Salvador

ARGENTINA

Rio Grande do Sul

Pôrto Alegre

URUGUAY

55°W

River Plate

© Oxford Cartographers

BRAZIL

Farmland & Forest

Highlands

★ Capital

● Major Cities

▲ Mountain Peaks

— Country Boundaries

0   100   200   300 Miles
0   200   400 Kilometers

5

WELCOME TO BRAZIL

Brazil is a very large country. It is the fifth-largest country in the world and has the fifth-largest population. Brazil covers almost half the continent of South America. Its borders touch ten other countries, including Argentina and Peru.

Brazil's eastern border is the Atlantic Ocean. This coastline is very long—4,347 miles (6,995 kilometers). Its western border is only a few hundred miles from the Pacific Ocean. Most of the country lies between the Equator, which runs through the north of Brazil, and the Tropic of Capricorn, which runs through the south. The climate of Brazil is mostly hot. The northeast is very dry, almost like a desert, but frosts are quite common in the south. South of the equator, most of the rain falls between December and April, which is Brazil's wet season.

The Amazon River flows eastward across northern Brazil. Smaller rivers from all the neighboring countries run into the Amazon. In the nearby rain forest there is a huge variety of plant and animal life. The rain forest is also home to many native tribes of Indians. The ancestors of these people were living in Brazil before settlers arrived from other countries.

▷ **The Amazon rain forest** Brazil has the world's largest rain forest. It surrounds the Amazon River. A quarter of all known types of plants are found here.

◁ **Street celebrations in Olinda, near Recife** Brazilians enjoy music, dance, and outdoor entertainment.

European explorers first landed on the coast of Brazil in 1500. They named the country after the brazilwood tree, which was especially valuable because of its red dye. Settlers from Portugal arrived and married the Indians already living there.

Rio de Janeiro was the capital of Brazil until 1960. Then it was replaced as capital by a new city, Brasília. This new city was built 620 miles (990 kilometers) from the coast, in an area where few people had ever lived.

▽ **Rio de Janeiro** Visitors can get an excellent view of the city from the cable car that goes to the top of Sugarloaf Mountain.

Brasília, the Modern Capital

President Juscelino Kubitschek was the man who did the most to create the new city of Brasília. He wanted a new capital city that would make use of unoccupied land in the middle of the country. It was also important for the capital to be within easy reach of the rest of the country.

A competition was held to choose the design for the new city. Professor Lúcio Costa won. His plan has been compared with the shape of an airplane. There is a very wide, long avenue like an airplane's body. All the government buildings stand on either side of this avenue. Homes, shops, and schools are built in areas shaped much like the airplane's wings. The city's bus station is located at the point where the wings meet the body.

The famous Brazilian architect Oscar Niemeyer designed the most important buildings. They include the Cathedral, the Congress Building, the President's Palace, and the Ministry of Foreign Affairs. Brasilia has been called the greatest city-building project of the twentieth century. Much of it was completed in five years, in time for the opening date of April 21, 1960.

A wood-carver At an open market in Brasília, a wood-carver is making a *carranca*—a head like the ones once used on boats on the São Francisco River.

The best view of Brasília is from the television tower. From here you look down the main avenue, the Eixo Monumental. Few people walk along this long avenue. The distances between buildings are great and the weather is very hot. Most people travel by car and bus on the city's excellent roads. More than two million people live in Brasília. Many of them work in government offices. But the city is often empty on the weekends. Many people still prefer to live in or near Rio de Janeiro. They stay in Brasília during the week to work.

◁ **The capital city** Brasília was built in the middle of the country. This wide avenue, the Eixo Monumental, is 5 miles (8 kilometers) long. The building at the far end is the Congress Building.

▷ **Brasília's cathedral** The roof has the shape of a "crown of thorns." The inside, shown here, is below the level of the sidewalk.

9

MINING COUNTRY

From Brasília it is a short flight to Belo Horizonte, the capital city of the neighboring state of Minas Gerais. The name Belo Horizonte means "Beautiful Horizon" in Portuguese. Minas Gerais means "General Mines." The name Minas Gerais comes from the huge amount of mineral wealth to be found in the region. It was this area of Brazil

▽ **The main square of Ouro Preto** On the tall pedestal is a statue of Tiradentes the Toothpuller, who led an unsuccessful revolt against the Portuguese in 1789.

that was first explored by pioneers, or *bandeirantes,* more than 200 years ago. They made their way slowly inland from the coast, searching for both gold and diamonds. They made friends with the Indians as they went and established trading posts. In the great gold rush that followed, prospectors arrived from all over Europe. During the 1700s, the mines of Minas Gerais provided nearly half of the world's gold and many of its diamonds.

The prospectors built beautiful colonial cities. Today you can visit some of these places close to Belo Horizonte. Ouro Preto and Congonhas are especially worth a visit. When trade was at its best, Ouro Preto had a population of 100,000. Both towns have fine churches and works by Brazil's famous colonial sculptor Antônio Francisco Lisboa. He was the son of a Portuguese architect and a black slave woman.

The statue in the main square of Ouro Preto is of Joaquim José da Silva Xavier, who was called Tiradentes, "the Toothpuller." He was a dentist who led a revolt fighting for independence from Portugal in 1789. The revolt failed and Tiradentes was executed.

Many of Brazil's minerals still come from Minas Gerais, but it is also very good country for cattle and for coffee. Coffee was introduced in Brazil in the 18th century. By the 1830s Brazil was producing nearly half of the world's supply. Coffee continues to be an important product for the country.

▷ **Coffee** Brazil grows more coffee plants than any other country. Here at harvest time the berries are being picked from the bushes by hand.

▽ **Ouro Preto** The name of this town means "Black Gold." It was founded in 1711, has 13 traditional churches, and is now a national monument.

FABULOUS RIO

The people of Rio are known as *Cariocas*. They say that God made the world in six days and the seventh he devoted to Rio de Janeiro. It is an astonishing city, especially seen from the air. As you fly over it, you will see the enormous Statue of Christ on Corcovado Mountain, the Sugarloaf Mountain in Botafogo Bay, and many other bays. You will also see offshore islands covered with forests. But do not be surprised if it is raining! This part of Brazil gets lots of rain.

Rio is famous for its beaches. Ipanema's beach features excellent hotels and restaurants nearby. On summer weekends the beach at Copacabana is so crowded that there is barely room to move.

Rio is also famous for Carnival and soccer. The Cariocas prepare for Carnival all year round, practicing samba dances. The dancers, or *sambistas*, make magnificent costumes. It is not just a parade. It is a serious competition to decide which samba school is best. Soccer, called *futebol*, is an even more serious matter. Everybody stops work when Brazil is playing in an important World Cup or international match. One of the world's largest soccer stadiums, the Maracanã, is in Rio. But any spare patch of ground serves as a field for young players. All young Brazilians hope that one day they will be as good as famous national soccer players Pelé and Ronaldinho.

On hillsides in and around the city are shantytowns where poor people live. Many thousands of people have come to Rio in recent years, looking for a better way of life. They want work, medical help, and schools for their children. But there is little work. Often children earn money in the streets by cleaning cars or running errands.

▷ **The greatest show on Earth** More than 80,000 dancers and 5,000 musicians take part in Carnival in Rio de Janeiro. During two nights of dancing, they compete to be the champions.

▷ **Favelas on a hillside**
These are the houses of the
poor people of Rio de Janeiro.

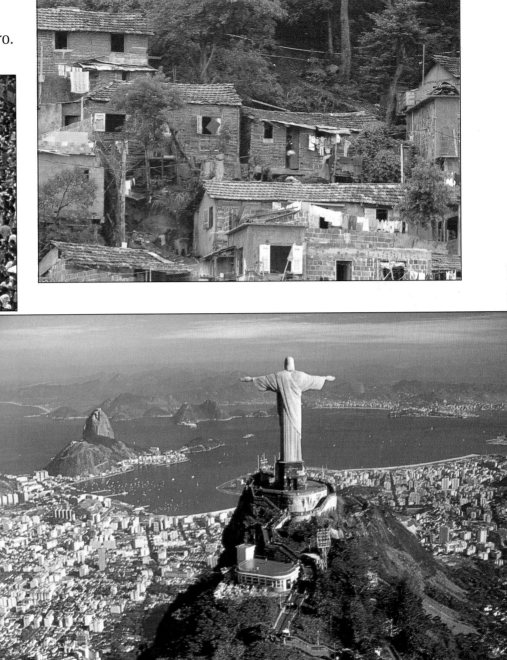

△ **Famous landmarks** Rio de Janeiro's most famous landmarks
are the huge statue of Christ the Redeemer and Sugarloaf
Mountain, seen here on the left.

13

CITY OF CONTRASTS

São Paulo is only about 260 miles (430 kilometers) south of Rio, but is a completely different kind of city. There are frequent air shuttle services between the two cities. But if you have time on your journey, travel instead on the old coastal road to Rio. Visit some of the pretty fishing villages and beautiful white sand beaches along the way.

Have a good map ready when you enter the city of São Paulo, or you may get lost. São Paulo is by far the largest city in Brazil and ranks among the world's top four in population. Finding your way through the maze of streets can be difficult.

Just over 100 years ago, São Paulo was a small settlement of about 30,000 people. Now it is Brazil's business center. The rapid growth of São Paulo began with the boom in the popularity of coffee. Millions of people from Europe, Japan, and other parts of the world came to live and work here. Today the state of São Paulo produces a fifth of Brazil's agricultural goods and well over half of its industrial goods.

The growth of the city has led to very bad pollution. Both the busy factories and the huge number of cars on the roads make the pollution worse. Even so, if you go up a tall building on a clear day, you can have a good view of the city. You look out over an amazing mass of skyscrapers crammed into the city center. The modern skyscrapers have replaced nearly all of the old buildings.

Beyond the center of the city are the areas where the homes of wealthy people are built. Here are some of South America's largest shopping centers and some of its most fashionable shops and restaurants. But tens of thousands of country people have also moved into São Paulo. They often have very poor homes in roughly built shanties.

△ **The bus terminal in São Paulo** Thousands of people arrive in São Paulo every day. Some of the new arrivals are tourists, but many others are Brazilians looking for work.

▷ **Families in São Paulo's shantytowns** Many homes have no water or electricity. Children spend much of their time playing in the streets.

▽ **São Paulo, the business center of Brazil** In the heart of the city, old buildings have been replaced by modern skyscrapers and apartments.

COWBOYS AND WATERFALLS

South of São Paulo are the three states of Rio Grande do Sul, Santa Catarina, and Paraná. The southernmost large city is Porto Alegre. This is a rich agricultural area. The far south, on the borders with Uruguay and Argentina, is cattle country. This is the land of the cowboys, or *gauchos*. They are easily recognized by their flat, black hats and baggy trousers. Gauchos herd millions of cattle on the vast grasslands. It is not surprising that meat is the most important part of any local meal. There are many restaurants where delicious *churrasco*, or barbecued meats, are served.

During the last hundred years, many settlers from northwest Europe have come to live in this region. Some villages are built in typical German style, with alpine wooden houses. In some places the people still speak German or Italian as their main language.

Curitiba is just like a European city. It has become well known recently as Brazil's first "green," or environmentally friendly, city. The city leaders are working hard to control traffic and pollution. They want to teach young children how to respect and care for natural resources.

Paraná State takes its name from the Paraná River. This major river forms part of Brazil's borders with Paraguay and Argentina. The magnificent Iguaçu Falls are on a small river that flows into the Paraná. The Itaipú Dam is on the main river, between Paraguay and Brazil. The Itaipú is one of the world's largest hydroelectric plants. It supplies electricity to São Paulo and many other cities.

▷ **The Iguaçu Falls** They are made up of more than 275 waterfalls and are one of the most spectacular sights in South America.

▷ **Children in a math lesson in a state school in the south** Brazilian children go to school from the age of seven.

▽ **An outdoor flower and plant market in Curitiba, the "green city"** The town hall overlooks the market.

THE HISTORIC CAPITAL

Salvador de Bahia is on Brazil's east coast, more than 1,000 miles (1,600 kilometers) to the north of Rio de Janeiro. The Portuguese colonists moved into this region first. They established sugar plantations here in the 1500s and 1600s.

Salvador grew wealthy and became the first capital city of Brazil. It was replaced as capital by Rio de Janeiro in 1763. The city is split into two levels connected by elevators and by a cable railway. Most of the colonial buildings are in the upper level. Here you will find glorious churches and monasteries, cobblestone streets and squares, pastel-painted houses, and the government palace.

Salvador de Bahia is more than just a reminder of colonial Brazil. It is also the heart of African Brazil. This dates from the 1700s, when people were brought from Africa as slaves to work on the plantations.

▷ **Workers collecting melons** Fruit growing along the São Francisco River has been made possible by irrigation.

Over time, African people and their culture mixed with the Brazilian population. African traditions became part of the local way of life. For example, *candomblé* is one of many religious cults. Bahiana women dressed in white chant and sway to the sounds of African music. The Festival of the goddess Yemanjá is especially interesting. Flowers and gifts are thrown into the sea for the goddess. African tradition also lives on in *capoeira*, a form of high-kicking martial arts dance.

An airplane ride from Salvador to the River São Francisco takes a little less than an hour. Brazilians think of the São Francisco as their national river, rather than the Amazon, because it begins and ends entirely within Brazil. The spectacular Paulo Alfonso Falls are 168 miles (270 kilometers) from the mouth of the river. The Paulo Alfonso Falls are now part of an irrigation plan that has made the dry land around them very good for farming. Some of Brazil's major oil fields are also in Bahia.

◁ **The Church of São Francisco, Salvador** The church, with its wonderful gold-leaf decorations, was completed in 1748.

▷ **Snacks from Bahia** In Salvador, a Bahiana woman sells African snacks made from beans, shrimps, palm oil, and coconut milk.

CATTLE, CRAFTS, AND COAST

North of Salvador is the poorest, hottest, and driest part of Brazil. The name *sertão* is given to the wild and barren inland regions of the northeast. Vegetation there, called *caatinga*, is mostly dry scrub brush and thorny bushes. Some palms, like the *babaçú*, produce valuable nuts and oils, but few other useful plants will grow in such a climate.

Most people here make a living raising cattle. It is a hard life for the cowboys of the northeast, the *vaqueiros*. They must live with the harsh weather and barren ground as they search for pasture for the herds.

△ **A family returning from market** Many families travel by horse or mule in the rural northeast and across the dry, empty *sertão*.

◁ **A market in Recife** Stalls are piled with pineapples, melons, grapes, brazil nuts, and locally grown palm fruit.

▷ **The village of Horto in the northeast** The streets are made of cobblestone and the houses are made of mudbrick and tile. Horto is in the center of a sugarcane-growing area.

The main towns of the northeast, such as Fortaleza, Recife, and São Luís, are on the coast. Recife is where the harvesting and export of brazilwood began. The nearby town of Olinda is sometimes described as the first capital of Brazil. This area is rich in crafts. Finely woven cotton hammocks, pottery, and wood carvings are among the many goods sold in the markets. There are also small clay figures modeled about local legends. One of these legends tells the story of Lampião. He was a cruel bandit who terrorized much of the northeast in the 1920s and 1930s.

The northeast region has some of the finest beaches in Brazil. Many new hotels are being built on the coast for tourists, but it is still sometimes possible to have a wonderful tropical beach all to yourself.

Toward late afternoon, try making your way to one of the small fishing villages along the coast. Here you can watch the small traditional *jangada* fishing boats bringing in the evening catch. Or you may prefer to make a trip inland to see the gigantic shrine of Padre Cícero. It honors a popular local priest who died in 1934.

THE MIGHTY AMAZON

The Amazon is one of the world's greatest rivers. It is 4,025 miles (6,437 kilometers) long and it flows through Brazil for almost half its length. The Amazon drains an area almost the size of the United States. Within Brazil alone, several hundred smaller rivers flow into the Amazon. The Amazon is the world's second-longest river. Only the Nile River in Africa is longer—by just 146 miles (234 kilometers).

The port of Belém is a good place to start a journey up the Amazon. But first, try to make a quick visit to Marajó. This large island is located at the mouth of the river. Then travel back to Belém to visit the *Ver o Peso*—the "see the weight" fish and fruit market on the dock. Here people sell huge Amazon catfish.

A riverboat will take you from Belém through narrow waterways into the main river. Then you travel onward 1,000 miles (1,600 kilometers) upstream to Manaus. For most of the journey the river is very wide. The rain forest looks like no more than a thin line on the horizon. From this distance you are not likely to see many land animals along the way.

▷ **The flooded forest** Parts of the Amazon rain forest are flooded for much of the year. People who live and work in this part of the forest go everywhere by boat.

22

◁ **The port of Manaus** Large ocean-going ships often come to Manaus, the largest city along the Amazon.

Manaus became a very important and wealthy city during the Amazon rubber boom about 100 years ago. At that time large quantities of rubber from the forests were exported for the auto industry. Much of the wealth is now gone, but grand buildings like the Opera House and the Customs House are still there. The Opera House, completed in 1896, was decorated with tiles from France, ironwork from Scotland, and paintings by Italian artists.

If you like adventure, you can take a boat trip from Manaus up the Rio Negro. You will see mountains with their tops in the clouds. Brazil's highest peak, the Pico da Neblina, is here.

▽ **Catfish for sale in the Manaus fish market** These huge fish can grow to 6 feet (2 meters) long and weigh 450 pounds (200 kilograms).

23

THE AMAZON RAIN FORESTS

From Manaus you can go on an expedition into the rain forest. But make sure you go with a guide. It is easy to get lost. Trails disappear between tall trees covered thickly in tropical plants and vines. The undergrowth is dense and leafy. There is not much wildlife close to the river, but deeper in the forest you may see colorful birds such as toucans and macaws. You may also see the tapir (the Amazon's heaviest animal), the capybara (the world's largest rodent), monkeys, and perhaps alligators.

Few people live in the forest. They are mostly rubber tappers or settlers. A few Indians still live there. Some live in lonely groups away from other people. Others live on the reserves organized by the government. Their way of life is still traditional. Their homes are made of palm and thatch. They have small gardens where they grow manioc, fruit, and vegetables. The appetizing dish *farofa* is made from manioc flour mixed with eggs and pieces of bacon. The Indians also hunt in the forest for meat. But their traditional way of life is threatened. The government has plans to cut large clearings in the forests so that timber can be sold, and much of the land continues to be used for farming, mining, and building.

Settlers from the coast and cattle ranchers can make profits from the forest land. During the last forty years, many new roads have been built. In 1967 a large deposit of iron was found at Carajás, not far from Belém. Dams have been built to provide electricity. All these changes have done terrible damage to the forest. Indians, rubber tappers, and land developers are now working out plans to protect the forests.

▷ **The iron ore mine at Carajás** This may be world's largest iron ore mine. Other minerals and metals are also found in the region. A specially built railroad takes the ore through the rain forest to the coast.

▷ **Gathering rubber** The Amazon rubber gatherer, or *seringueiro*, makes slashes in the trunk of the tree. He collects the latex, or sap, in a cup. The latex is then smoked over a fire and turned into large balls ready for transport down the river to the port.

▽ **Chief Raoni, leader of the Kayapó Indians** Chief Raoni became well known when he joined Sting, the popular musician, to tell people about damage done to the rain forest.

THE CENTRAL STATES

The states of Mato Grosso, Mato Grosso do Sul, Goiás, and Tocantins lie south of the Amazon and cover a large area in the center of Brazil. Most of the people here live and work in the main cities of Goiânia, Cuiabá, Campo Grande, and Corumbá. Corumbá is the main border town with Bolivia.

Very few people live in the rest of the land, but there are some native tribes here. They are in danger of losing their homes as business leaders buy the forest land. They hope to make profits from it or to find gold.

Among the most interesting places to visit here are the national parks with their wonderful variety of wildlife. The national parks can be difficult to reach, but seeing them is well worth the effort. The central-western plains, known as the Pantanal, are especially interesting. The animals and plants there are like those near the Amazon. They are easier to see here because the land is more open. Experts believe that 650 species of birds and 230 species of fish may live there. Many water birds, such as herons and ibises, and the flesh-eating piranha fish, are found in this region. There are also many alligators. Although it is against the law, poachers still hunt alligators.

There is more to see on the island of Bananal in Tocantins. Many of South America's unusual mammals, like the maned wolf and giant anteater, are found on the island.

Goiás State is one of Brazil's fastest developing farming areas. The crops are rice, coffee, and soybeans. Cattle are also raised here. Until 1960, when the Federal District was created, Brasília was part of Goiás. To end your journey through Brazil, you can join the Trans-Amazonian Highway, which runs from Belém through Goiás to Brasília.

▽ **Across the Mato Grosso**
An interstate highway links the cities of Campo Grande and Cuiabá. It crosses a part of Brazil where very few people live.

△ **A farm worker's home**
A farm worker, his wife, and seven children live in this typical wooden homestead.

▽ **Cattle and cowboys** Cattle are raised on the vast ranches in Goiás and Mato Grosso by cowboys, who spend days out in the open with the herds.

BRAZIL FACTS AND FIGURES

People

Most Brazilians are of mixed origins. Some are *mestiços*, descended from European and native Indian marriages. Others are *mulatos*, who have African and European ancestors. Today there are probably between a total of 100,000 and 150,000 Indians left in the country.

Settlers also came from many European countries and Japan.

Trade and Industry

Brazil is thought to be one of the world's largest sources of iron ore. In addition, Brazil is one of the world's leading producers of ethanol, which is made from sugarcane. Most vehicles in the country are fueled by either ethanol or gasohol, a mixture of ethanol and gasoline.

Brazil is the third-largest producer of oil in Latin America. Most of the oil fields are in the northeast and offshore. Brazil also has plentiful electricity supplied by dams.

Factories have been built mainly in the São Paulo region. Vehicles, chemicals, processed foods, and textiles are among the variety of goods they produce.

△ **A *Bahiana* dressed for Carnival in Rio de Janeiro** Bahianas are Brazilians of African descent from the northern state of Bahia.

Fishing

Fish is an important source of food and the catch includes cod, crab, lobster, and shrimp. Fishing provides a livelihood for many coastal villages and for groups of people living along the riverbanks deeper inside the country.

Although Brazil's coastline is very long, its commercial fishing industry is quite small.

Farming

Brazil is the world's largest producer of coffee and one of the largest producers of sugarcane. Coffee is grown in central and southern states. But in some years harvests have been lost due to frosts. Sugarcane is an important crop in many parts of Brazil. Brazil is one of the world's biggest producers of soybeans. It also supplies most of the world's orange juice.

Other crops sold abroad are tobacco, cocoa, and cotton. Staple foods for the home market include rice, potatoes, manioc, beans, and maize.

Most of the biggest cattle ranches are in the southern part of the country. Cattle are raised for dairy products and beef. Most is used in Brazil itself.

Forestry

Brazil may have as much as one-third of the world's timber. Hardwoods such as mahogany are highly valued and come from the rain forest. Paraná pine and other softwoods grown in the south are used to make furniture and paper.

Food

Many Brazilians regard *feijoada* as the national dish. The main ingredients are black beans with dried and smoked meats, for example beef, tongue, bacon, and sausages. This is served with side dishes of rice, *farofa* (manioc flour mixed with eggs and bacon), and oranges.

In Bahia, African-style food is hot and spicy and almost always includes *dendê* oil from a local palm. A typical dish is *moqueca*—seafood cooked in coconut milk, herbs, tomatoes, peppers, and dendê.

Fish, particularly large catfish, is the main food in the Amazon region. In the south no meal is complete without beef. And there is fresh fruit of every kind. Juice bars are popular in many cities.

A favorite drink is *cafezinho*, strong, black, sweet coffee.

Schools

Schools in Brazil are run by the State, by the Church, or are paid for privately. By law, all children have to go to primary school from the age of seven to fourteen.

△ **Timber to send abroad** Mahogany from Brazil is highly valued by furniture makers around the world. The timber is obtained from trees growing in the rain forest.

But many do not attend school because they live far away from the main towns and cities, and there is no school to go to. Others stay home because the family needs them to work.

Only a small number of children go on to secondary school and very few to university. About 86 percent of Brazil's population can read and write.

The Media

There are more than 250 TV stations in Brazil, but the largest is TV Globo, which often has audiences of more than eighty million. Satellite TV is now seen all over Brazil and used for education. There are also over 1,000 radio stations.

Brazil has more than 250 daily newspapers. The main papers are *O Globo* and *Jornal do Brazil* in Rio de Janeiro, and *O Estado de São Paulo* and *Folha de São Paulo* published in São Paulo. English and foreign language newspapers are available from Europe and the U.S. Rio has its own English-language newspaper.

Art

Brazil's best-known modern artist is Candido Portinari. Many of his paintings show local scenes, such as people working on coffee plantations.

Brazil's twentieth-century sculptors include Alfredo Ceschiatti and Bruno Giorgi. Their work, for example Giorgi's *Statue of the Warriors*, can be seen in Brasília. It stands next to the modern buildings that were designed by Lúcio Costa and Oscar Niemeyer.

29

Brazil Facts and Figures

Music

Brazilian music has its origins in Portuguese, African, and Indian cultures. Instruments include guitars and accordions in the south, the one-string *berimbau* from Bahia, and pipes and drums from the native tribes.

The samba is the best-known dance. There are also many folk dances. The lambada is a very popular dance in the north.

Religion

More than 70 percent of Brazilians are Roman Catholic, the religion introduced by the Portugese priests and missionaries. About 15 percent of Brazilians are Protestant. Some people are followers of traditional African religions such as *candomblé*, *macumba*, and *umbanda*. The Indians worship their own gods and spirits.

Festivals and Holidays

Many of Brazil's national festivals and holidays are part of the religious calendar. Towns and villages hold their own saints' days.

The main national holidays are:
February or March **Carnival**
April 21 **Tiradentes Day** Named

△ **The Toco toucan** This is one of the most colorful birds of the South American forests.

for the day of the execution of the rebel leader José Xavier
June **Corpus Christi**
September 7 **Independence Day** Celebrates independence in 1822
November 2 **All Souls' Day** A day in memory of the dead
November 15 **Day of the Republic** Commemorates the day the country was proclaimed a republic in 1889

Sports

The most popular game in Brazil is *futebol*, or soccer. The national team has played in all World Cup Finals, and it has won five times—a world record.

Three Brazilians have been World Formula One Grand Prix Champions: Ayrton Senna (tragically killed in 1994), Nelson Piquet in the 1980s, and Emerson Fittipaldi in the 1970s. In 2016, Rio de Janeiro will host the Summer Olympics. It will be the first South American city ever to host the games.

Plants and Animals

Useful plants growing in the rain forest include brazil nuts and palms, which produce oil, fibers, and fruits. Other fruits are *maracujá*, or passionfruit, and *açaí*, used as a flavoring for ice cream.

The rain forests are home to such animals as poisonous tree frogs, sloths, hummingbirds, capuchin monkeys, and jaguars.

The United Nations Earth Summit Conference, during which world leaders discussed care of the environment, was held in Rio de Janeiro in 1992.

HISTORY

The original native peoples of Brazil lived in the forest, hunting and fishing. The Portuguese sailor Pedro Alvarez Cabral was the first European to land there, in 1500. Brazil was a Portuguese colony for about 300 years.

In 1789 the first revolt against the Portuguese crown, led by Joaquim José da Silva Xavier, or *Tiradentes*, failed. Then, early in the 19th century in Europe, the French threatened to invade Portugal. The Portuguese king, Dom João, moved his court to Brazil. Dom João remained in Brazil for sixteen years before returning to Portugal. When he left Brazil, his son, Dom Pedro, became ruler of the country.

The Portuguese government demanded the return of Dom Pedro, but he refused. On September 7, 1822, he declared Brazil's independence. Three months later, Dom Pedro was crowned emperor. He was not a good ruler, and in 1831 he resigned. He left his son, Dom Pedro II, in charge. Dom Pedro II was crowned emperor of Brazil in 1840 at the age of fifteen.

Dom Pedro II was successful in a war against Paraguay. But he was removed from office and sent into exile in 1889. Brazil became a republic. Under the presidency of Getúlio Vargas (1930–1945), the living standards of the people improved. Under president Juscelino Kubitscek in the 1950s, and then under the rule of a military government in the 1970s, massive spending on buildings left Brazil deep in debt.

After years of troubles, the 21st century has brought Brazil a new government and fresh hope.

LANGUAGE

Portuguese is the official language of Brazil. It is different from European Portuguese because many of the words come from indigenous languages. Many of the Indian tribes have kept their own languages.

Many immigrants from Europe and the east also continue to use their own languages, especially the Japanese and the German communities in the south.

Most Brazilians understand a Spanish speaker, but it is not always easy to understand the Portuguese reply.

Useful words and phrases

English	Portuguese
One	*um*
Two	*dois*
Three	*três*
Four	*quatro*
Five	*cinco*
Six	*seis*
Seven	*sete*
Eight	*oito*
Nine	*nove*
Ten	*dez*
Sunday	*domingo*
Monday	*segunda-feira*
Tuesday	*terça-feira*
Wednesday	*quarta-feira*

Useful words and phrases

English	Portuguese
Thursday	*quinta-feira*
Friday	*sexta-feira*
Saturday	*sabado*
Good morning	*Bom dia*
Good afternoon	*Boa tarde*
Good night	*Boa noite*
Good-bye	*Tchau*
Very good	*Muito bom*
Please	*Por favor*
Thank you	*Obrigado*
Yes	*Sim*
No	*Não*
Do you speak English?	*Fala inglês?*

INDEX

Book created for Highlights for Children, Inc.
by Bender Richardson White.
Editors: Peter MacDonald and Lionel Bender
Designer: Malcolm Smythe
Art Editor: Ben White
Editorial Assistant: Madeleine Samuel
Picture Researcher: Annabel Ossel
Production: Kim Richardson

Maps produced by Oxford Cartographers, England.
Currency from MRI Bankers Guide to Foreign Currency.
Stamps courtesy Scott Publishing Co., Sidney, OH
45365 (www.scottonline.com).

Editorial Consultant: Andrew Gutelle
Guide to Brazil is approved by the Brazilian Embassy, London
Brazilian Consultant:s: David Lorimer and Deborah P. da Costa, São Paulo
Managing Editor, Highlights New Products: Margie Hayes Richmond

Picture Credits
SAP = South American Pictures, TM = Tony Morrison, Z = Zefa. t = top, b = bottom, l = left, r = right.
Cover: Z. Pages: 6-7: TM/SAP. 7t: TM/SAP. 7b: Mark Downey/Lucid Images. 8, 9t, 9b:TM/SAP. 10, 11t, 11b: TM/SAP. 12-13: Z/Veiga Leal. 13t: TM/SAP. 13b: Z/Richard Steedman. 14: TM/SAP. 15t: Eye Ubiquitous/Daniel Jungman. 15b: David Frazier. 16-17, 17b: TM/SAP. 17t: Eye Ubiquitous/Julia Waterlow. 18, 19t, 19b: TM/SAP. 20b, 20t, 21: TM/SAP. 22-23, 23t, 23b: TM/SAP. 24-25: TM/SAP. 25t: Edward Parker/SAP. 25b: Bill Leinbach/SAP. 26-27: Edward Parker/SAP. 27t, 27b: TM/SAP. 28, 29, 30: TM/SAP. Illustration on page 1 by Tom Powers.